The HEALTHY
**green**
DRINK Diet

Skyhorse Publishing books may be purchased in bulk at special discounts for sales promotion, corporate gifts, fund-raising, or educational purposes. Special editions can also be created to specifications. For details, contact the Special Sales Department, Skyhorse Publishing, 307 West 36th Street, 11th Floor, New York, NY 10018 or info@skyhorsepublishing.com.

Skyhorse® and Skyhorse Publishing® are registered trademarks of Skyhorse Publishing, Inc.®, a Delaware corporation.

Visit our website at www.skyhorsepublishing.com.

10 9 8 7

Library of Congress Cataloging-in-Publication Data is available on file.

ISBN: 978-1-61608-473-8

Printed in China

# The HEALTHY green DRINK Diet

## Advice and Recipes for Happy Juicing

JASON MANHEIM
Photography by Leo Quijano II

Skyhorse Publishing

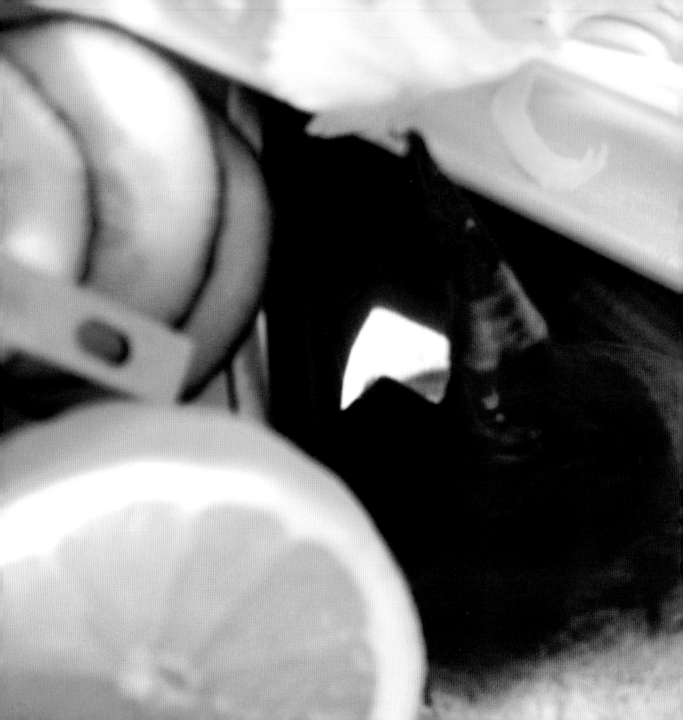

CONTENTS

# Introduction

# The Green Drink Diet

# SMOOTHIES

# JUICES

# Introduction

*Every human being is the author of his own health or disease.*
—Siddhārtha Gautama

This book is not for vegetarians. It is not for vegans, raw foodists, meat eaters, or Paleo eaters. It is for people—everyone—far and wide, no matter your current eating practices. It is for people who struggle, day to day, to find the "right" way to manage *life* and *health*. Mothers, fathers, children, athletes, business people, the common folk, royalty, the infirm . . . this book is for all of you. It is a key step in taking your health by the reins and finally claiming responsibility and know-how for your own well-being. The best way to do that is to give you something you can measure.

We eat healthy because we want to feel healthy—fantasies of living *longer* should not trump the importance of living *stronger*. Although there have been numerous studies outlining the therapeutic effects of diet on illnesses like cancer, heart disease, and immune disorders, we cannot let that obscure our motivation—the simple fact that eating good feels good.

Despite the title suggesting *diet*, this book is more of a supplement to the diet you already enjoy. It is my belief that adding "good" foods to your diet is a more efficient way of reaching goals than taking away "bad" foods. Whether you want to lose weight, fight fatigue, combat disease, or just be healthier, adding green drinks will slowly replace your bad habits and transform your health for the better. Not only that, but this process retains healthy eating practices long after the motivation of trying a completely new system has worn off.

With all of that in mind, this book has one very simple goal: eat at least one green drink a day, preferably before a meal. That's it. From there, it's up to you how far you take it. Optimally, I suggest two to three per day, before your biggest meals. But once a day is a great place to start.

## The Author

I am first and foremost, just a nerd with an insatiable appetite for knowledge. I love exploring new ways to push my body to extremes while still maintaining a healthy foundation. Over the years, I've studied and converted to more diet fads and fitness programs than I can remember. I've also worked as a certified personal trainer and slowly learned what works, and what doesn't.

In early 2008 I started healthygreendrink.com, with the premise of documenting the green drinks I consumed on a daily basis. To be honest, all I really wanted to do was teach myself how to rank in search engines for certain keywords. The website and web development in general, slowly became another one of those obsessions that claims every speck of my free time. But, it paid off. My lifelong obsession with health and fitness helped me turn my dabbling in web development into a way to share one of my other passions, green drinks.

The process of picking a topic and squeezing every bit of information out of it as I can makes it easy for me come up with ways to make the information digestible— and that's what I've done here.

I'm dedicated to the never-ending process of learning and pushing the boundaries of that knowledge in order to share what I have learned along the way. Nothing I've ever done has proven to be more beneficial to my overall health than what is provided in the following pages. It's easy, delicious, and anybody can do it.

You are the author of your own health, so let's give you what you need to know.

# Why Go Green?

Often used to signify nature, fertility, prosperity, growth, renewal, freshness, harmony, youth, conservation, energy, balance, and well-being, *green* is akin to life itself. It's no wonder the greatest food a person can ingest is, well, *greens*.

But like I said previously, this book is not concerned with preaching a specific diet like vegetarianism or veganism. Truth be told, I lean toward the Paleolithic diet more than anything else. Green drinks supplement whatever diet you have already chosen. Luckily, they're greeted with open arms by vegetarians, vegans, meat-eaters, Paleo eaters, and Zone diet practitioners alike. No one, it seems, can dispute the health benefits of eating greens.

## *Protein*

First, let's put that "but I need protein" argument to rest. Whether or not you eat meat doesn't really matter. Plants, despite what you may have heard, can give you all the protein you need. Which, according to the Institute of Medicine's (IOM) *Dietary Reference Intakes for Energy, Carbohydrate, Fiber, Fat, Fatty Acids, Cholesterol, Protein, and Amino Acids,* is about 50 grams per day for the average adult. A better way to gauge this is to make sure 10 to 20 percent of your total food intake consists of protein.

Proteins are made up of twenty amino acids, nine of which are known as *essential* because the body cannot make them and therefore requires them from food sources. You may have heard the argument that animal protein is a "complete" protein and vegetable protein is "incomplete," however that isn't exactly true. According to the same report, a protein is said to be "complete" if the nine essential amino acids make up these percentages of the protein being eaten:

| Tryptophan | 0.7 | Threonine | 2.7 | Isoleucine | 2.5 |
|---|---|---|---|---|---|
| Leucine | 5.5 | Lysine | 5.1 | Valine | 3.2 |
| Arginine | 1.8 | Methionine+Cystine | 2.5 | Phenylalanine+Tyrosine | 4.7 |

Since most of us eat a varied diet, and the green drinks we're going to make use a wide variety of leafy greens, fruits, and other superfoods, there are absolutely no issues with hitting those numbers and more. Not to mention, most green vegetables *do* contain all nine amino acids, just not in the amounts that make them "complete."

Furthermore, many prominent experts still insist that vegans combine foods at every meal to make up for the so-called "incomplete" proteins. This is an absurd notion. We don't have to eat an optimum amount of any other nutrient at every meal in order for our bodies to use them properly, so why do we have to combine foods to complete the amino acid chains? We don't. As long as we eat a variety of fruits and vegetables, we have nothing to worry about proteinwise.

# Vitamins, Enzymes, Minerals, Fiber, and More . . .

Greens are the most nutritionally dense foods on the planet; they're very low in calories and pack one helluva nutrient punch. They're high in antioxidants; carotonoids; flavinoids; vitamins A, C, E; folic acid, and calcium among a myriad of other vitamins and minerals. They're also packed with dietary fiber that won't irritate your body's digestive system like other fibers. Since most people on a typical American diet are grossly deficient in fiber, green drinks are a fast and easy way to put that problem away for good.

All of these nutrients protect from an almost staggering amount of ailments like the following:

- heart disease
- cancer
- skin conditions (eczema, psoriasis . . . )
- high blood pressure
- high cholesterol
- bacterial growth
- viral growth
- tumors
- asthma
- headaches
- insomnia
- bladder infections
- bowel issues (IBS, celiac disease . . . )

# Alkalize, Lose Weight, Fight Fatigue

Greens are a very alkaline food and can help regulate your blood to a healthier alkaline (as opposed to acidic) state. Disease and destruction occur more readily in a body that is mostly acidic (also known as *acidosis*).

This alkaline state, along with the vast nutrient content of greens, plays a vital role in your body's ability to metabolize and distribute fat correctly and can increase your ability to lose weight significantly. It also gives you a boost of energy and begins training your body to fight off fatigue. If your body is busy fighting disease all day, it's no wonder you're tired all the time. Alkalize your blood, get your vitamins and minerals, and enjoy your newfound energy.

A quick note—lemons and limes, although one would think would be acidic, actually have an alkaline effect on the body, so don't worry about adding a few squeezes to your green drinks, it will only amplify the alkalizing effects.

For more information regarding pH and the benefits of an alkaline diet, I suggest you read *The pH Miracle* by Robert O. Young, Ph.D.

## *More Reasons . . .*

- For years I battled with acid indigestion and something I can't diagnose as anything other than a weak stomach. Instead of ending my days with a nice glass of tea and a good book, I was regularly propped upright in bed waiting for the heartburn medication to kick in. Those of you who suffer from the fire within know that most remedies don't work. Sleeping standing up? Nope. I fell over. Drinking a glass of milk? Just adds inches to my waste. Aloe vera juice? A little, but mostly just has a laxative effect. *Gaviscon*? Yes! These foamy pills do the trick, but how do I prevent it from ever happening in the first place? Nothing I did ever *prevented* my acid reflux until I introduced a change to my overall diet. Green drinks. It began changing the pH of my body, neutralizing the acids responsible for the reflux, and after a few months, it even allowed me to eat the occasional pastrami sandwich piled high with mustard without the slightest burning. I've been relatively heartburn free ever since.

- You'll eat a wider variety of greens than you ever have before with greater ease than you ever thought possible. I don't know about you, but I can't remember the last time I had a plate of turnip greens and Swiss chard. But I do remember the last time I blended some up . . . this morning!

- Blender blades are better than your teeth at breaking down cell walls of fruits and greens thereby releasing a greater amount of vitamins, minerals, and enzymes. And juicing is even better than that if you fork out the cash for a triturating juicer. We're talking enzyme-city.

# The Greens

*Variety is the very spice of life, That gives it all its flavor.*

—from *The Task* (1785) by William Cowper

Variety is also the key to optimal health. In order to enjoy the most complete nutrition, it's important to consume a wide variety of greens. It ensures our bodies receive ample amounts of one nutrient and doesn't overdo it on another, all the while keeping our taste buds from shorting out due to boredom. A great way of achieving this is to eat with the seasons; if it's not available, don't eat it until it is. Experiment, mix it up, try new things . . . it's good for you!

The following list consists of the main leafy greens used throughout this book and in my very own kitchen. You will find a brief table listing the nutrient contents for each green and a short description outlining the major nutritional benefits, flavor profiles, and ways of incorporating them into your own green drinks and smoothies.

## *Arugula (Rocket)*

2 cups (40 g), raw

| | | |
|---|---|---|
| 1.03 g protein | .6 g fiber | 64 mg calcium |
| .58 mg iron | 148mg potassium | 11 mg sodium |
| 949 IU vita A | .034 mg riboflavin | .029 mg vita B6 |
| 6 mg vita C | .17 mg vita E | .043 mg vita K |

This peppery, mustard-flavored dark leafy green is part of the cruciferous family of vegetables (like broccoli, cauliflower, brussels sprouts), which makes it a potent anticancer food. It's very aromatic, so be careful what you mix it with as it can easily dominate the flavor of your drink. To combat that effect, you can use baby arugula because of its milder flavor. It's so easy to grow; you can plant a few seeds in a pot by the window and enjoy it year-round. Arugula is also a noted aphrodisiac, so don't skimp and share, share, share. It's a great source of calcium; vitamins A, C, K; and potassium as well.

## Basil

5 leaves (2.5 g), raw

| | | |
|---|---|---|
| .08 g protein | 0 g fiber | 4 mg calcium |
| .08 mg iron | 7 mg potassium | 0 mg sodium |
| 132 IU vita A | .002 mg riboflavin | .004 mg vita B6 |
| .5 mg vita C | .02 mg vita E | .01 mg vita K |

One of the most common herbs used in cuisines around the world; basil is often used as a natural anti-inflammatory and an inhibitor of bacterial growth—great for those with inflammatory bowel conditions and arthritis. I love basil. It's another one of those fragrant, easy-to-grow, year-round pleasures. There are over sixty varieties of basil so experiment; each one differs slightly in appearance and taste. It's a fantastic source of vitamin K and also includes good amounts of iron, calcium, and vitamin A.

# Beet Greens

2 cups (76 g), raw

| | | |
|---|---|---|
| 1.67 g protein | 2.8 g fiber | 89 mg calcium |
| 1.95 mg iron | 579 mg potassium | 172 mg sodium |
| 4808 IU vita A | .167 mg riboflavin | .081 mg vita B6 |
| 22.8 mg vita C | 1.14 mg vita E | .3 mg vita K |

Most people go right for the root and toss the tops. Stop! They're delicious, rich in vitamin K, folate, magnese, and fiber. Not only that, but they taste very similar to the root, so you won't be missing much. If you're growing your own beets, you can pull a few leaves off each plant while letting the root continue to grow. The folate content is great for lowering LDL cholesterol, and the red pigment is known to raise antioxidant enzymes in the liver. Blend the greens and juice the roots—it's a perfect duo.

# Bok Choy

2 cups chopped (140 g), raw

| | | |
|---|---|---|
| 2.1 g protein | 1.4 g fiber | 147 mg calcium |
| 1.12 mg iron | 353 mg potassium | 91 mg sodium |
| 6255 IU vita A | .098 mg riboflavin | .272 mg vita B-6 |
| 63 mg vita C | .13 mg vita E | .06 mg vita K |

Here's another one of those cancer-fighting cruciferous greens. They're very mild in flavor, and although technically a cabbage, it's less dense and much leafier than other cabbages, so feel free to pack them in the blender as it won't leave you with that chunkiness you sometimes get from solid cabbage. Full of powerful antioxidants and beta-carotene.

## *Broccoli*

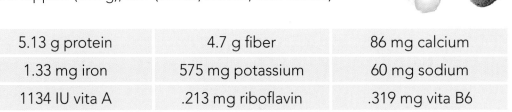

2 cups chopped (182 g), raw (stems, leaves, and flower)

| 5.13 g protein | 4.7 g fiber | 86 mg calcium |
|---|---|---|
| 1.33 mg iron | 575 mg potassium | 60 mg sodium |
| 1134 IU vita A | .213 mg riboflavin | .319 mg vita B6 |
| 162.3 mg vita C | 1.42 mg vita E | .19 mg vita K |

Here we are, King Cruciferous . . . or cancer's *kryptonite*, as I like to call it. Think of a malady, any malady, and I'm willing to bet the health benefits of broccoli have been known to combat it. Things like diabetes, Alzheimer's, stomach, breast, lung and colon cancer, heart disease, arthritis, and more. You can even eat the stems, just make sure to peel away the harder parts. It's overflowing with vitamins C, K, and A, folate, and fiber. You can also try broccoli rabe, which is a bitter-tasting brother to broccoli.

# Cabbage

2 cups chopped (178 g), raw (common green variety)

| | | |
|---|---|---|
| 2.28 g protein | 4.5 g fiber | 71 mg calcium |
| .84 mg iron | 303 mg potassium | 32 mg sodium |
| 174 IU vita A | .071 mg riboflavin | .221 mg vita B6 |
| 65.1 mg vita C | .27 mg vita E | .14 mg vita K |

Again with the cruciferous? Cancer doesn't stand a chance. A great source of vitamin K and C, cabbage comes in many different shapes and sizes. Red, green, Savoy (curly), Napa (or Chinese cabbage), even brussels sprouts and bok choy are types of cabbage. In the Middle Ages, this humble leaf ball was known as the "drug of the poor" because it was cheap, and a diet rich in it cured most ailments. Cabbage juice has been quite effective at preventing and curing stomach ulcers because of its fantastic anti-inflammatory properties.

# Celery

2 medium stalks (80 g), raw

| | | |
|---|---|---|
| .55 g protein | 1.3 g fiber | 32 mg calcium |
| .16 mg iron | 208 mg potassium | 64 mg sodium |
| 359 IU vita A | .046 mg riboflavin | .059 mg vita B6 |
| 2.5 mg vita C | .22 mg vita E | .023 mg vita K |

Celery belongs to the same family as fennel and parsley and gives your smoothies a slightly salty taste. It pairs beautifully with sweet fruits like apples. Careful how many stalks you fill your blender with when making smoothies as all but the most powerful blenders have trouble breaking down its stringiness; great for juicing, though. It's rich in vitamins K and C and is a great immune system booster. Celery also has the potential for reducing high blood pressure because of compounds called phthalides, which allow blood vessels to dilate.

## Chard

2 cups (72 g), raw

| 1.3 g protein | 1.2 g fiber | 37 mg calcium |
|---|---|---|
| 1.3 mg iron | 273 mg potassium | 153 mg sodium |
| 4404 IU vita A | .065 mg riboflavin | .071 mg vita B6 |
| 21.6 mg vita C | 1.36 mg vita E | .6 mg vita K |

Brimming with vitamins A, C, and K, this leafy green has been known to also regulate blood sugar levels and provide anti-inflammatory benefits due to its high phytonutrient content. It is next to spinach for denseness of nutrients, so don't skimp. It's a beautiful green leaf with many different varieties to try: rainbow, Swiss, red, golden, and white. Along with mustard greens, kale, and collards, chard is one of the four leafy green vegetables commonly referred to as "greens."

# Cilantro (Coriander)

1 cup leaves (16 g), raw

| | | |
|---|---|---|
| .34 g protein | .4 g fiber | 11 mg calcium |
| .28 mg iron | 83 mg potassium | 7 mg sodium |
| 1080 IU vita A | .026 mg riboflavin | .024 mg vita B6 |
| 4.3 mg vita C | .40 mg vita E | .05 mg vita K |

This fragrant herb has somewhat of an acquired taste but has been used to treat a multitude of problems like reliving intestinal gas and aiding digestion, calming inflammation due to arthritis, and lowering blood sugar and LDL cholesterol. It's also been used effectively to fight Salmonella. I use it sparingly and mostly to add a little kick in flavor. It pairs well with citrus, spiciness, and fruits like mango.

# Collards

2 cups chopped (72 g), raw

| | | |
|---|---|---|
| 1.76 g protein | 2.6 g fiber | 104 mg calcium |
| .14 mg iron | 122 mg potassium | 14 mg sodium |
| 4801 IU vita A | .094 mg riboflavin | .119 mg vita B6 |
| 25.4 mg vita C | 1.63 mg vita E | .37 mg vita K |

You thought we were done with the cruciferous family, didn't you? Collards are one of the best cholesterol-lowering foods known to man and is practically overflowing with vitamins A, C, and K, manganese, folate, calcium, and dietary fiber. It's got a bit of spiciness to it but otherwise pretty mild in terms of flavor. It goes well with basil and strawberries. Next time you're mixing up a big pot of overcooked collards and bacon grease, save a few fresh leaves and try it in Strawberry Patch.

## *Dandelion Greens*

2 cups chopped (110 g), raw

| | | |
|---|---|---|
| 2.97 g protein | 3.9 g fiber | 206 mg calcium |
| 3.41 mg iron | 437 mg potassium | 84 mg sodium |
| 11177 IU vita A | .29 mg riboflavin | .28 mg vita B6 |
| 38.5 mg vita C | 3.78 mg vita E | .86 mg vita K |

They may take over your garden and cause you to go on a picking rampage but don't throw them out, they're rich in vitamins A and K and are known to have purifying effects on the blood and liver. Unfortunately, you can't pack these greens in the blender like you would with something like spinach . . . unless you have a taste for the extremely bitter. It's better combined with other greens and a few sweet fruits, or if you can find them or pick them young, they're much less bitter. Note: if you're picking these from your yard, make sure they're pesticide free.

# Kale

2 cups chopped (134 g), raw

| | | |
|---|---|---|
| 4.42 g protein | 2.7 g fiber | 181 mg calcium |
| 2.28 mg iron | 599 mg potassium | 58 mg sodium |
| 20604 IU vita A | .174 mg riboflavin | .363 mg vita B6 |
| 160.8 mg vita C | ~ vita E | 1.1 mg vita K |

This cold,hardy, green leafy powerhouse of nutrients is, you guessed it, another member of the cruciferous family. If broccoli is the king, kale is the king's hand. Full of vitamins A, C, and K, kale is also a powerful weapon against bladder, breast, colon, ovary, and prostate cancer. It can be a tough one for some blenders due to its waxy texture, so be sure to blend until the chunks go away. It's a mild-flavored green, slightly bitter, and can be found in many varieties; try black lacinato (dino), curly (Scotch), Napus, blue leaf, red leaf, and white leaf.

# Lettuce (Mixed Greens)

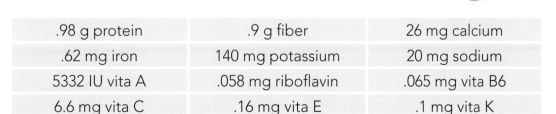

2 cups shredded (72 g), raw (green leaf)

| | | |
|---|---|---|
| .98 g protein | .9 g fiber | 26 mg calcium |
| .62 mg iron | 140 mg potassium | 20 mg sodium |
| 5332 IU vita A | .058 mg riboflavin | .065 mg vita B6 |
| 6.6 mg vita C | .16 mg vita E | .1 mg vita K |

The nutrient table above is specifically for green leaf lettuce; however, throughout this book, I simply refer to lettuce as any combination of mixed green you usually find prepackaged in bags at your local market. Sometimes called mesclun (baby greens), it can consist of green leaf lettuce, red leaf lettuce, endive, frisée, radicchio, oak leaf, iceberg, mache, mizuna, and romaine. Generally speaking, the darker and more colorful the lettuce, the more nutritious. Fill your drinks with as much variety as possible.

## *Mint*

1 cup chopped (26 g), raw

| | | |
|---|---|---|
| .96 g protein | 2 g fiber | 62 mg calcium |
| 1.3 mg iron | 146 mg potassium | 8 mg sodium |
| 1087 IU vita A | .068 mg riboflavin | .033 mg vita B6 |
| 8.1 mg vita C | ~ vita E | ~ vita K |

Easy to grow throughout the year, mint is good for more than just a soothing winter tea or invigorating summer beverage. Many studies have shown mint to be a fantastic remedy for upset stomachs from ailment such as IBS, indigestion, and other colonic issues. It gives any drink a burst of refreshing flavor, and the aroma can even cure nausea and headaches.

# Mustard Greens

2 cups chopped (112 g), raw

| | | |
|---|---|---|
| 3.02 g protein | 3.7 g fiber | 115 mg calcium |
| 1.64 mg iron | 396 mg potassium | 28 mg sodium |
| 11760 IU vita A | .123 mg riboflavin | .202 mg vita B6 |
| 78.4 mg vita C | 2.25 mg vita E | .56 mg vita K |

Hello, cruciferous vegetable, long time no see. Mustard greens are a great addition to your detox regime; it contains many antioxidant nutrients and phytonutrients that help the body eliminate unwanted toxins. Be warned, though, these leafy greens have a spicy, tangy punch that will leave you chasing with cold water. Best mixed with less bold greens and a few sweet fruits.

# Parsley

2 cups chopped (120 g), raw

| | | |
|---|---|---|
| 3.56 g protein | 4 g fiber | 166 mg calcium |
| 7.44 mg iron | 665 mg potassium | 67 mg sodium |
| 10109 IU vita A | .118 mg riboflavin | .108 mg vita B6 |
| 159.6 mg vita C | .9 mg vita E | 1.97 mg vita K |

Not just a table garnish, folks. The oils in parsley can neutralize some carcinogens and is a great source of folic acid, which keeps your heart functioning healthily and it combats colon and cervix cancer. It really brings out the flavors of other ingredients and is especially tasty with celery and tomatoes. It also lasts much longer than other greens when you store it in a plastic bag in the refrigerator.

## *Spinach*

2 cups (60 g), raw

| | | |
|---|---|---|
| 1.72 g protein | 1.3 g fiber | 59 mg calcium |
| 1.63 mg iron | 335 mg potassium | 47 mg sodium |
| 5626 IU vita A | .113 mg riboflavin | .117 mg vita B6 |
| 16.9 mg vita C | 1.22 mg vita E | .29 mg vita K |

Known as one of the world's healthiest vegetables, it's no wonder Popeye was able to defeat Bluto time and time again. Spinach is rich in vitamins A, C, B2, B6, E, and K, manganese, folate, magnesium, iron, calcium, and potassium. Spinach is also nearly 50 percent protein. However, due to the oxalic acid, which can combine with metals in the body and irritate the kidneys, it is recommended to get a wide variety of leafy greens and not depend on spinach alone. Despite that, and because I have a diet high in liquids which flushes the majority of metal compounds in by body, it's my go-to green and can be added to any drink without compromising flavor. I usually stock my fridge with bags of it from Trader Joe's. Because of the mild flavor and texture, kids and green drink novices love it too.

# Turnip Greens

2 cups chopped (110 g), raw

| | | |
|---|---|---|
| 1.65 g protein | 3.5 g fiber | 209 mg calcium |
| 1.21 mg iron | 326 mg potassium | 44 mg sodium |
| 12746 IU vita A | .110 mg riboflavin | .29 mg vita B6 |
| 66 mg vita C | 3.15 mg vita E | .28 mg vita K |

I like to think of these as stage one mustard greens. They're pungent and a bit spicy but won't have you running for a glass of water like mustard greens do. They're a great source of vitamins A, C, and K, folate and fiber. Like mustard greens, they're great for detox support, are rich in antioxidants, and provide anti-inflammatory benefits. It's a great way to add some new greens while providing a flavorful punch.

# Watercress

2 cups chopped (68 g), raw

| | | |
|---|---|---|
| 1.56 g protein | .3 g fiber | 82 mg calcium |
| .14 mg iron | 224 mg potassium | 28 mg sodium |
| 2170 IU vita A | .082 mg riboflavin | .088 mg vita B6 |
| 29.2 mg vita C | .68 mg vita E | .17 mg vita K |

Historically, watercress has been praised for its healing properties. In fact, it's said that Hippocrates, the father of Western medicine, built his hospital near a stream so he could have access to fresh watercress while treating the sick. It's high in vitamins A, C, and beta-carotene and has been shown to reduce DNA damage in white blood cells. It's mildly bitter and spicy, and I usually use it as a substitute for wheatgrass when I don't want to bother juicing it.

## Other Greens, Lettuces, Weeds, and Veggies

**Tarragon**          **Mizuna**          **Fennel**

Try some of the following to add a bit of variety to your smoothies and juices:

| | | |
|---|---|---|
| fresh tarragon | kohlrabi tops | carrot tops |
| anise/fennel | purslane | lamb's-quarter |
| radish | green onion | fresh oregano |
| mizuna | radicchio | beets |
| | brussels sprouts | |

# Adding Fruit

By now you have at least *tried* a green drink, right? Let me guess, something with 90 percent fruit and 10 percent greens and you loved it? . . . You're not alone. Most people start off that way, after all, eating something sweet is much easier than trying to gulp down a glass of whipped bitter greens when you're not used to it. However, here's where I bum you out a bit and make your adoption of the Green Drink Diet a bit more challenging: fruit is full of sugar. Fructose to be specific.

That's not to say that fruit isn't healthy, it is. In fact, aside from greens, fruits have the most vitamins and minerals pound for pound than any other food. But if your goal is weight loss and possibly lowering your cholesterol, then limiting your fructose consumption is probably a good idea. Studies have shown that diets high in fat, as commonly thought, are not the main culprit of weight gain and high LDL cholesterol, sugar is.

That being said, there's nothing wrong with a little fruit in your diet, especially for those attempting to transition into a more greencentric supplemental drink or those transitioning out of a more processed Americanized diet.

Fresh berries are a staple in my smoothie regimen, specifically blueberries for their antioxidant properties and because sometimes I prefer a blue tinge to the

radioactive green. Another staple is bananas; not for any nutritional benefit, (although they are high in potassium and fiber), but because they pull the smoothies together. They bind flavors and give the drink a delicious creamy texture.

Like the greens, use these when in season to sweeten your green drinks, enhance flavor, and add a nutritional boost:

- apricot
- apple
- avocado
- banana
- bell pepper
- blackberries
- blueberries
- cherries
- cantaloupe
- cranberries
- cucumber
- grapes
- grapefruit
- guava

- honeydew melon
- kiwi
- kumquat
- lemon
- limes
- mango
- nectarine
- orange
- papaya
- pear
- peach
- persimmon
- pineapple
- plums

- raspberries
- star fruit
- strawberries
- tangerine
- tomato
- watermelon

# Adding "Superfoods"

These aren't your typical superfoods so don't panic, we're not going to blend a fresh-caught wild Alaskan salmon with a head of broccoli. These are "extras" that are packed with nutrition and are perfect for blending (or juicing). Whether adding healthy fats, fibrous seeds, or vitamin-dense berries, the green drink is an easy way to incorporate them when you otherwise might not have.

Some of these are quite expensive and some require additional time spent cultivating, so use as sparingly or as much as you see fit.

## Acai Berries

The acai berry (pronounced "ah-sigh-EE") comes from the acai palm and is native to Central and South America. I'm sure you have heard of them, though, they're all the rage in the health food circuit at the moment. They're extremely high in antioxidants like anthocyanins and flavonoids. Anthocyanins are what gives fruit and vegetables those darker blue, red, and purple hues and help the body fight free radicals and defend against aging, heart disease, and cancer. Try to find these either whole or mashed in the frozen section of your local health food store. Skip the juices and tonics as they're usually full of other additives.

# Almond Butter

Almonds are high in monounsaturated fats, which promote lower LDL cholesterol and reduce the risk of heart disease, lower blood pressure, and control blood sugar. Not to mention they're delicious and add a light nutty flavor and creamy texture to your green smoothies. Look for raw, salt-free varieties.

# Aloe Vera

Aloe vera is a succulent plant commonly used as a topical agent to treat minor burns. Its immune-stimulating effects don't stop there, though, it can reduce symptoms associated with psoriasis and eczema, and can be a fantastic way to detox the colon. However, be careful how much you add because it's also a natural laxative; you want to detox, not spend hours stuck to the toilet. As an added bonus, it's one of the few plant sources of vitamin B12, so, vegans, take note. Try growing your own plant as the nutrition is better or look for pure (meat included, sugar-free) juice at your local health food store.

# Avocado

Often called the "food of the gods," and for good reason. It's one of the healthiest sources of monounsaturated fats you can eat. When added to your green drink, it can increase absorption of the carotenoid antioxidants lycopene and beta-carotene up to 300 percent. It's also known for its anti-inflammatory properties. Try adding some to your green smoothies for a thicker, more flavorful drink.

## Bee Pollen

Bee pollen is a mixture of flower pollen, nectar, and enzymes secreted by bees. It's commonly used by athletes for increasing energy, stamina, and endurance. Long-term effects are weight loss, enhancement of the immune system, improved sexual function, and seasonal allergy relief. Try buying bee pollen gathered from multiple sources as it increases the nutritional benefit and the allergy relief properties. And of course, if you're sensitive to pollens, test the waters first before jumping straight in.

## Cayenne Pepper

Not only does it add flavor and heat to your drink, capsaicin, the substance responsible for the spiciness, can have pain-reducing effects, improve cardiovascular health, prevent ulcers, and clear up those nasal passages. Be very careful, though—a shaky hand can leave you submerging your head in a bucket of ice water.

## Chocolate (Raw)

Stay away from the checkout stand, you won't find the kind of chocolate I'm talking about there. This chocolate is raw and additive- and sweetener-free. It's rather expensive but is high in antioxidants and can lower blood pressure. The most important benefit? Taste! Add a few organic raw cocoa nibs to your shake with a slice or two of avocado and you'll have yourself a very tasty, nutritious treat.

## Coconut (Oil, Milk, Water, Meat)

The coconut is one of nature's miracle foods. It's used for skin care as a moisturizer, to prevent heart disease, for utilizing lauric acid which lowers blood pressure and cholesterol levels, for weight loss by increasing the bodies metabolism, and so much more. It's even used in hospitals on patients with digestive problems and is a primary ingredient in most infant formulas. I like adding fresh young coconut flesh and water to my green smoothies whenever possible. If you're adding coconut oil, let it melt first before adding it to the blender; that way you won't get the waxy film and chunkiness you get from the solid oil.

## Flaxseed (Oil, Seeds)

Flaxseeds are high in alpha-linolenic acid (ALA), an essential omega-3 fatty acid which is a precursor to the much-touted omega-3s found in fish oils (EPA). The body naturally converts ALA to EPA, so flaxseed is a great alternative to fish oil, especially for vegans. Omega-3s have been known to have incredible anti-inflammatory properties; protect bone health; protect against heart disease, cancer, and diabetes; and prevent and control high blood pressure. Flaxseed oil goes rancid fast, so buy only the fresh, refrigerated bottles at your local health food store. You can also use a coffee grinder to grind your own whole flaxseeds, adding a textural difference to your smoothies as well.

## Garlic

Garlic contains many sulfur compounds that promote cardiovascular health, prevent blood clotting, lower blood pressure, and have tremendous antibacterial and antiviral benefits. It has also been shown to improve out iron metabolism. Because of its potent flavor, I suggest no more than one small clove per drink, and sometimes even less than that. Build your tolerance; don't ruin it by overdoing it from the start.

## Ginger

This stem can add quite a spicy flavor boost to your green smoothies. Ginger is prized for its ability to prevent motion sickness, eliminate digestive issues, prevent nausea and vomiting during pregnancy, and its many anti-inflammatory effects. I keep a big piece in my freezer at all times and add it to my smoothies whenever possible; just peel the outer layer off with a sharp knife and zest a bunch right into the blender or slice off a thumb-sized piece from a fresh piece for juicing.

## Pumpkin

The alpha-carotene, beta-carotene, and vitamin E in pumpkin make for a fantastic healthy skin supplement and the heavy fiber content protects from heart disease, promotes healthy digestion, and controls blood sugar levels. Fresh pumpkins are a bit tough to deal with, so I like to use Libby's 100 percent Pure Pumpkin. It comes in a can, and you can find it in the baking section of most grocery stores. Add a tablespoon or two to any green smoothie as a boost to your daily skin regime. Naturally, it goes well with a bit of fresh ground cinnamon and nutmeg.

# Sprouts

Broccoli, radish, fenugreek, alfalfa, clover, and bean sprouts are all easy to grow, full of nutrition, and a great addition to any green drink. They're mini versions of the larger vegetables and living powerhouses of vitamins, minerals, and enzymes. There are plenty of places online that offer high-quality seeds and sprouting kits, so do some research and try for yourself. I like Sprout People (http://sproutpeople. org/), they've been around for a long time and have fantastic kits for beginners.

# Wheatgrass

Liquid energy. Wheatgrass is so nutrient-rich that 30 mls (~1 oz.) is equivalent in nutritional value to 1 kg. (~2.2 lbs.) of leafy green veggies. Because wheatgrass is made up of 70 percent chlorophyll, it increases the body's production of red blood cells, lowers blood pressure, stimulates healthy tissue growth, and breaks down carbon dioxide. I've seen shriveled old men turn into princes on this stuff. You can try blending the whole grass if you have a very high-powered blender, but the texture is still a bit weird for me (plus, humans have a hard time digesting wheatgrass due to its fibrous nature), so I recommend juicing the grass and adding it to your smoothies after they've been blended. You can also use organic wheatgrass powder, but try to use fresh when possible.

# Sweeteners (If You Must)

Those of you using a good amount of fruits in your green drinks won't have much of a need to sweeten them even more, but sometimes a stronger sweet-kick is in order. For instance, anything with pumpkin and cinnamon could use a few dates or a spoonful or two of honey . . . you know, just to get that pumpkin pie effect.

If you've read the intro under "Adding Fruit," you know I don't have much room in my heart for processed sugars, so this section only provides fresh, natural sweeteners despite the food industries' fascination with trying to create the next "sugar" that doesn't inevitably kill you.

The list is short and sweet . . . use sparingly.

## *Agave Nectar*

Agave nectar is produced from the agave plant, which is not a cactus but in fact is succulent like aloe and is the same plant responsible for your college hangovers (tequila!). The best thing about agave nectar is its low glycemic index compared to sugar or honey, yet it's significantly sweeter. Use raw, organic agave nectar that has been cold-processed to reduce enzyme destruction. A teaspoon or two will do.

## Dates

As the oldest cultivated fruit, dates have an even lower glycemic load than agave and are high in potassium, magnesium, selenium, and calcium. I can eat these things until I pass out, they're so delicious. Toss a few into your green smoothies (don't forget to remove the pits) and bask in the sweet, ancient glory of the date.

## Honey

Okay, we're done with the low glycemic load stuff, so those with blood sugar issues need not apply. Honey is the greatest invention ever created by the combined efforts of flowers and bees and has a slightly increased sweetness factor than granulated sugar. Unlike granulated sugar, honey contains minerals, vitamins, pollen, and protein. The pollen can even help combat your seasonal allergies. Get some from your local farmer's market. Like agave nectar, a teaspoon or two will do.

The HEALTHY **green** DRINK Diet

# Tips: Buying, Saving, Growing, and Storing

## *Buying*

In order of most desirable to least desirable, these are the places you should purchase your fresh fruits and veggies:

- Local farmer's market—these places are a fruit and vegetable wonderland. It's straight from the local farms so you can't get any fresher than that. Try to find one that specializes in organic food and start a relationship with a few producers; they'll start saving you good stuff and offer great discounts.

- Small local market—there are quite a few small, family-owned Asian and Mexican markets in my area that sell produce from local farms. There prices are generally cheaper than big grocery stores, and the variety is more diverse. Seek these places out, they're worth it.

- Grocery store—Nowadays, big grocery stores have a small organic produce section; however, the fruits and veggies are almost always wilted and starting to go bad. Your best bet is the nonorganic stuff. Purchase here only when the sales are unbeatable and you can't get to a farmers market or small local market.

Look for vibrant colors, crisp leaves, and stout, strong stalks. Keep away from anything wilted or overly pungent and also greens that are dry and yellowing. And always buy organic when possible.

Some studies have shown organic produce to contain higher amounts of nutrition while other studies have seen no significant increase. Either way, organic fruits and veggies contain, at most, pesticides derived from natural sources rather than the carcinogenic pesticides that are synthetically manufactured, and that's reason enough to make the switch. Granted, organic is often more expensive, but if you stick to locally grown produce from farmer's markets and small local stores, there are generally deals to be had.

## *Saving*

Start buying your most used greens in bulk. I like to stock up on spinach by buying huge prewashed bags at places like Costco or Trader Joe's. Also, consider purchasing your berries in large frozen bags and buying bananas in bulk (freezing them before they get too ripe). These are all much less expensive than purchasing in smaller quantities.

You can even freeze your spinach if the giant bag proves to be difficult to consume before going bad. All of this is going to add some weight to your freezer, so I recommend a second deep freezer in the garage, storage shed, or patio.

And then, of course, you can grow your own greens . . .

# *Growing*

This is easier than you think, even for those of you living in apartments with no backyard access. At the very least, all you need is a windowsill that gets a good amount of sunlight. Not only is it easy, but it's the cheapest way to get your green drink fix.

Here are three important steps to get you started:

- Seeds—talk to the suppliers at your local farmer's market or search online for open-pollinated, nonhybrid, natural, non-GMO seeds. I like to use www. rareseeds.com (they have a very wide variety) or www.sproutpeople.org (they specialize in sprouts).

- Equipment—check your local home improvement store for planters in a variety of sizes, pick up some wood if you want to build your own grow box (I recommend reading *All New Square Foot Gardening* by Mel Bartholomew if your space is limited), purchase a sprouting kit (I recommend www.sproutpeople. org), and don't forget the fertilizer and manure.

- Space—grow in windowsills, patios, yards, porches, hanging baskets, the walkway on the side of your house or apartment, homemade grow boxes, the list is endless. You can even rent a space from your city's community gardening location.

I suggest starting with a few herbs like basil and mint and a few easy leafy greens like spinach and lettuce of any variety. Kale, strawberries, tomatoes, beets, chard, and carrots are also easy to grow if you have the space.

Try adding some onions, marigolds, garlic, and hot peppers to keep the pests away. You can also purchase ladybugs from your local nursery to rid yourself of aphids, or do what my grandmother used to do and mix a bit of natural dish soap with water in a spray bottle and douse your plants to keep the critters away.

There's nothing like keeping your own fresh edible garden, so give it a try and reap the benefits.

## *Storing*

Fresh fruits and greens last on average about one week. Here are some tips to extend that time for as long as possible:

• Don't prewash your fruits greens. If you do, you'll find then molding, getting soggy, and wilting much faster.

• Store your greens, unwashed, in sealed plastic bags to keep out air and water.

• Keep most fruits (except citrus) on the countertop and out of the refrigerator; otherwise, you'll end up with mealy fruit. Avocados can be ripened on the counter and stored in the refrigerator to slow the process.

- Store cut fruit in a sealed plastic bag to prevent it from absorbing weird refrigerator smells.

- If something can't be eaten before going bad, chop it up, put it in a sealable bag, and toss it into the freezer.

- Fresh basil and other herbs can be stored in the refrigerator wrapped in a slightly damp paper towel, or you can freeze them in ice cube trays covered with water—a great way to chill your smoothies and get some extra flavor and nutrition.

# The Green Drink Diet

## Think *Supplement*, Not *Diet*

Most diets will have you rummaging through your refrigerator and cabinets looking for "bad" foods to fill your garbage can with. This won't. In fact, keep those Twinkies, I guarantee you'll throw them out of your own accord once your body adopts the green drink.

Here's what you do:

- Tomorrow morning, before breakfast, try one of the green drinks in this book.

- Do it again the next day before breakfast. And again the day after that until a full week has gone by.

That's it, you ask? That's it. After the first week of drinking green, if your body doesn't feel better, stronger, and crave the nutrition it provides, well then no book or amount of steps is going to convince you. But I believe in the power of what you can feel, and there's no doubt that the green drink makes you feel better than you ever have before.

I often find myself thinking (despite the morbidity) that I eat a particular meal or food item because when my peers are trading in their walking shoes for bed-pans and suffering from clogged arteries, cancer-laden organs, and old-age, I'll be cartwheeling into my golden years, disease-free and alive as ever. This thinking is not only gloomy but downright wrong in terms of inspiring repetitive healthy eating practices—I should instead focus on the measurable facts, and so should you. Although living longer and preventing diseases like cancer are fantastic bonuses to maintaining a healthy diet, they cannot provide short-term, measurable results—and let's face it, in our digital world of instant gratification, we want something that we can see or feel *now*.

Imagine eating an entire head of broccoli, a handful of blueberries, a spoonful of raw almond butter, and an apple all whipped up into a delicious smoothie . . . you can't *feel* your body *not* getting cancer; you can't *feel* your life span lengthening . . . but you can feel your energy levels increase, your focus intensify, your hunger satiate, and your body shift into overdrive—ready to take on any task you can throw at it. These are measurable, motivational, and gratifying results that you feel almost instantly—and it's all you need to make eating healthier a core component of your diet. Best of all, this is easy; gulping down a huge percentage of your daily nutrients in one fell swoop is a lot less time consuming than trying to put together and then *eat* an enormous salad.

# Making Your Green Drink: Equipment and How-To

The single most worthwhile purchase I have ever made (aside from my iMac) is my Blendtec Total Blender; it's powerful and looks fantastic. I recommend either a Vitamix or Blendtec for the serious green drinker, and since I've owned both I can honestly say the differences are negligible. Although, if for some reason you need to blend a few golf balls or a brick, go with the Blendtec (www.willitblend.com).

As for juicing, I own a Breville Ikon Juice Extractor. It's a centrifugal juicer, which means it grinds the fruits and veggies and spins the juice through a mesh strainer at very high speeds. This causes a bit more oxidation that the purist might scoff at, but since I drink the juice right away, it doesn't pose a problem for me. Most juicers on the market are centrifugal.

There are also masticating juicers which chew the fruit and vegetable fibers at lower speeds, causing less oxidation and producing more enzymes, vitamins, and fiber. The best type of juicer is called a triturating (twin gear) juicer. It operates at the slowest speed so oxidation is hardley an issue at all and has a two-step process. First it crushes the fruits and greens and then it presses them. As you can imagine, triturating juicers are quite expensive.

There are also specialized juicers specifically for wheatgrass; however, most masticating and triturating juicers can handle wheatgrass as well. Since I only use a centrifugal juicer, I get my freshly squeezed wheatgrass from either my local Sunday farmer's market or my local Robeks.

It's important to note that the lower the speed, the better in terms of nutrients. Significant oxidation (oxygen causing the fruits and greens to decompose) occurs when green drinks are blended and to a lesser degree when juiced. A triturating juicer causes the least amount of oxidation and is highly recommended to those with serious health concerns.

I juice a lot less than I blend. In fact, I make a green smoothie at least once a day and regulate juicing to when I need a quick pick-me-up or need to get rid of expiring fruits and vegetables. If I'm honest, it's a time thing. Juicing takes a lot of cleaning, assembling, and disassembling while blending is quick and easy.

These recipes are a great starting place, and once you've learned the combinations you prefer, you can begin to experiment.

My morning smoothie routine normally looks like this:

- Fill the blender a quarter of the way with water or coconut water.
- Add some frozen berries (whatever I have in the freezer).
- Grab two giant handfuls of greens (whatever I have in the refrigerator).
- Add a spoonful of raw almond butter or Libby's Pumpkin.

- Melt a big tablespoon of coconut oil in the microwave for thirty seconds and add it to the blender.
- Blend.

Break this down into the template I spoke of and you have this:

- Add some water.
- Add fruit.
- Add greens.
- Add superfoods.
- Blend.

For newbies and children, start with a higher percentage of fruits and slowly add more and more greens until you're ready to turn that sweet tooth into a green tooth. Also, skip the uncommon greens and stick with spinach until your (or your kids') palate adjusts.

It can't get any easier than that. Be creative, try new things, experiment, and find what strikes your fancy.

# Juicing vs. Blending

You'll notice the recipes are split into two sections, smoothies and juices. But which is better? I'll keep this simple:

## *Juicing Benefits*

- Less oxidation. Ever notice how a cut apple turns brown after leaving it on the counter for a while? That's called oxidation, and it's the process of decomposition. The fruit is actually starting to decompose and naturally, the nutrients are beginning to as well. Blending whips significant amounts of air into the drink in order to work and therefore exposes the drink to a greater amount of oxidation. For the least amount of oxidation, get a slow-speed triturating juicer.

- Quick nutritional boost. Since all the fiber is removed, the vitamin, enzymes, and minerals in the juice enter your bloodstream almost immediately after consumption.

- Quick energy boost. Due to the quick nutrient boost, your body is instantly refreshed and revitalized.

- Easily digestible. Because the fiber is removed, the body has an easy time digesting the remaining nutrients. It's great for quick cleanses and those with digestive issues.

- No bloating and heaviness. A full glass of juice will leave feeling light on your feet and won't ruin your appetite. It'll just keep you from stuffing your face with that extra taco.

## *Blending Benefits*

- Less sugar. Juicing ten apples will yield a significantly less amount of drink than blending ten apples. It's easier to consume a much larger amount of fructose when juicing.

- More fiber. Blending your fruits and greens retains all that good digestive system cleaning fiber.

- It's a complete meal. You've got your vitamins, minerals, enzymes, fiber, protein, and even fat if you add some avocado or coconut oil. You can even add superfoods like nut butter.

- Easier cleanup. Juicers usually require taking apart the whole thing and cleaning the pulp mess. Blending is a simple rinse-and-store.

SMOOTHIES

# A Grape Pear

## Ingredients

1 cup green grapes
1 pear
1 cup kale
1 orange (peeled)
1 banana (optional)
water/ice

Fill blender with as much water/ice as you like and add kale. Blend until smooth. Add fruit. Pulse blend until desired consistency.

*A grape . . . I mean, great one for the novice green drinker. The pear, grapes, orange, and banana make for a sweet-enough smoothie while still providing the nutritional benefits from the kale.*

*Due to the waxy nature of kale, it's best to use a high-powered blender like a Vitamix or Blendtec. If using a standard-powered blender, be sure to blend the kale and water longer.*

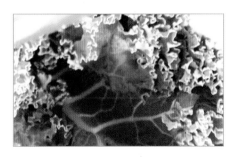

# Apple Raz

## Ingredients

1 red apple
1 cup fresh raspberries
⅛ honeydew melon
1 big kale leaf (remove stem)
1 handful baby greens
1 lemon (juice)
1 banana (optional)
water/ice

Fill blender with water/ice, add kale, greens, and apple. Blend until smooth. Add remaining ingredients. Pulse-blend until desired consistency.

*The sweetness of the red apple and the sour tang of the fresh raspberries and lemon balance out the bold flavor of the calcium-rich kale. Baby greens add a boost of vitamins and really makes this a well-rounded green drink.*

*A great way to kick off your morning!*

# The Healthy Green Drink

## Ingredients

1 bunch watercress
1 green apple
1 lime (peeled)
¼ English cucumber
4 mint leaves
1 banana (optional)
water/ice

Fill blender with as much water/ice as you like and add ingredients. Blend until smooth.

As the title track in our album of health, the Healthy Green Drink is a powerhouse of nutrition and taste.

Watercress, which can be commonly found at local farmer's markets and grocery stores, is often overlooked. It adds a wonderful spiciness while the mint-cucumber combination cools it down. A refreshing accompaniment to any meal.

# Just Peachy

## Ingredients

**4 whole peaches**
**1–2 cups spinach**
**water/ice**

Fill blender with as much water/ice as you like and add ingredients. Blend until smooth.

*Here's a simple one. Great for kids and those having trouble incorporating greens into their diets.*

*Spinach really packs a punch. It's a common green; you can get it just about anywhere, it's affordable, and the taste is mild enough that anyone can enjoy it. It's a great source of iron and beta-carotene and protects from a multitude of maladies. And who doesn't like peaches?*

# Mango Mint-jito

## Ingredients

1 cup mango
2 cups lettuce greens
5 large mint leaves
½ lemon (juice)
½ lime (juice)
1 banana (optional)
water/ice

Fill blender with as much water/ice as you like, adding mint and greens. Blend until smooth. Add fruit. Pulse-blend until desired consistency.

*For the lush in all of us. Except, you know . . . without all the stumbling and liver damage. In fact, with the amount of fiber and enzymes in mangoes, you can lower LDL cholesterol and improve digestion.*

*A fresher, healthier approach to its boozier counterpart, the Mango Mint-jitos' sweet tropical flavors will leave you hungry for a day by the pool instead of a night hugging the toilet.*

# Strawberry Patch

## Ingredients

3 strawberries
1 mango
1 kiwi
3 big basil leaves
2 large collard leaves
(remove stems)
water

Fill blender with as much water as you like, adding collard greens and basil. Blend until smooth. Add fruit. Pulse-blend until desired consistency.

A sweet treat and an easy way to introduce dark greens like collards into your diet. Collards have a strong, distinct flavor especially when cooked, but when blended raw among earthy-sweet and tropical flavors like kiwi and strawberry, you'll find collards are great at adding a spicy zing to an otherwise typical fruit smoothie.

Mangoes add a list of health benefits to the smoothie with enzymes that aid healthy digestion, glutamine for memory power, and heart-healthy antioxidants.

# Straw-megranate

## Ingredients

6 strawberries
1 cup pomegranate seeds
1 red apple
1 stalk celery
1 peach
1 handful red grapes
2 handfuls fresh spinach
1 banana (optional)
water

Fill blender with as much water as you like. And ingredients. Blend until smooth.

*Big, bold strawberry flavor with a tarty pomegranate kick. This antioxidant-rich smoothie may decrease the risk of heart disease and guard against free-radical damage.*

*Blending pomegranate seeds can be tough for some blenders, so if you're not rocking a Vitamix or Blendtec, try replacing them with some fresh-squeezed juice or a cup of store-bought pomegranate juice.*

# Black Melon

## Ingredients

½ cup watermelon
½ cup honeydew melon
½ cup cantaloupe
½ cup blackberries
2 handfuls fresh spinach
1 banana (optional)
water/ice

Fill blender with as much water/ice as you like, adding greens. Blend until smooth. Add fruit. Pulse-blend until desired consistency.

*An easy way to start introducing greens into your smoothies is to start off sweet. This drink is higher in natural sugars but still provides essential nutrients without the added preservatives and refined sugars. Black Melon contains high amounts of antioxidants, fiber, and vitamin C.*

*Spinach, an amazing source of protein, has a very subtle flavor and is often completely masked by any sweetness from fruit. Taking care of your body has never tasted so good.*

# Green Java

## Ingredients

1 bunch wheatgrass
2 oranges (peeled)
1 banana (optional)
water/ice

Fill blender with as much water/ice as you like, adding wheatgrass (if you don't have a high-powered blender, juice the wheatgrass first). Blend until smooth. Add fruit. Pulse-blend until desired consistency.

*Some of us can't even function until we get our morning coffee. A quick jolt of caffeine and energy is all you need, but what you tend to get is high calories, excess sugar, and a tainted smile. Hardly appealing when you can get twice the energy boost with none of those downfalls in a glass of wheatgrass-heavy Green Java.*

*Blend juiced wheatgrass with orange and banana to cut the bite of wheatgrass's intense flavor and pump you full of vitamin C and potassium.*

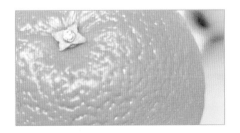

# Aloeberry

## Ingredients

1–2 large spears fresh aloe
    vera (or ¼ cup bottled)
1 cup spinach
2 large leaves chard
1 green apple (seeded)
1 cup frozen blueberries
1 banana (optional)

Fill blender with as much
water/ice as you like,
adding first 4 ingredients.
Blend until smooth. Add
fruit. Pulse-blend until desired consistency.

*If you're looking to get more vitamin B12 in your diet without significant meat intake, aloe vera is one of the only suppliers of vitamin B12 that doesn't come from animal products.*

*Chard is also a great source of omega-3 fatty acids if you're not the biggest fan of fish or eggs. Aloeberry has a little bit of everything for the vegans out there looking to avoid vitamin deficiency while still delivering an all-around great taste and healthful experience.*

# Tropical Sun

## Ingredients

2 bulbs bok choy
1 orange (peeled)
1 cup coconut water
1 cup pineapple
1 banana

Add first 3 ingredients. Blend until smooth. Add fruit. Pulse-blend until desired consistency.

*You may not be able to make it to the tropics before breakfast, but you can sure make it to the blender to make yourself this delicious flavor getaway.*

*Before your daily grind starts, treat yourself to the rich vitamins orange and pineapple have to offer. Bok choy, categorized as a negative-calorie food by its ability to facilitate the burning of calories, tastes amazing alongside its tropical components. Throw in a tiny umbrella for good measure and you won't be missing any nutrients; all you'll be missing is the beach.*

# Anti-toxi-mint

## Ingredients

4–5 mint leaves
½ English cucumber
2 large leaves collard
   greens
½ cup frozen acai berries
1 kiwi (peeled)
1 lemon (juiced)

Add first 3 ingredients.
Blend until smooth. Add
fruit. Pulse-blend until desired consistency.

*Perfect for you trend dieters out there looking for better skin, antiaging properties, cancer fighters, and improving cognitive brain function. Truth be told, all greens can deliver these same benefits, but that's just not what the beauty magazines are about these days.*

*Even still, you can't beat the tart and tangy taste the Anti-toxi-mint delivers while still being the tabloid starlet who can do anything and everything (even help prevent cancer) and taste good doing it.*

# Sweet Potato Pie

## Ingredients

1 cup semi-cooked sweet
   potato (or ½ juiced)
1 tbsp. ground flax
½ fennel/anise bulb
1 orange (peeled)
2 cups spinach
1–2 fresh figs
1 cup coconut water
cinnamon to taste

Add all ingredients. Blend until smooth, adding water as necessary.

*Even if autumn is not quite yet in the air, you can bring the nostalgia and flavors of the season into your morning smoothies or have it as dessert. Sweet potatoes are a nutritional superstar that are high in dietary fibers, beta-carotene, and complex carbohydrates and are known to improve blood sugar regulation and digestion.*

*Fennel, while adding a warm licorice flavor, is also good for digestive health and often used to combat bad breath. Ground flaxseed is rich in omega-3 fatty acids, high in fiber, and adds a nutty element, all together giving you a tasty, low-starch, guilt-free take on a classic seasonal dessert.*

# Just Beet It

## Ingredients

1 medium beet (skinned
    and chopped into
    chunks)
2 cups arugula
1 red apple
4–5 leaves basil
1 banana

Add all ingredients. Blend
until smooth, adding water
as necessary.

*Dance around your kitchen and tell coffee cakes
and pantry snacks to take a hike now that you're
on the road to a healthier you. Or you can let
your actions speak louder than words and blend
up a glass of Just Beet It.*

*Beets are essential for heart health and have an
earthy-sweet taste. Arugula contains antiviral
and antibacterial properties as well as high levels
of vitamin K. Though it's known to have a bitter
taste, when paired with an apple and banana,
there's nothing bitter . . . or should I say better.*

# Dumpkin Pie

## Ingredients

1 cup pumpkin (either
fresh or canned)
2 tbsp. raw almond butter
2 cups spinach
1 cup frozen blueberries
1 banana
cinnamon or nutmeg to
taste

Add all ingredients. Blend
until smooth, adding water
as necessary.

*This is it, folks, my go-to green smoothie. I can be a bit vain, so I add as much skin-regenerative pumpkin as I can stomach. The raw almond butter adds a dose of healthy fats, and the spinach and blueberries give me all the protein, vitamins, and antioxidants I need.*

*Cinnamon turns this strange concoction into something deliciously "pie-latable" rather than a patch of discarded pumpkins decomposing at the local dump. It's Dumpkin Pie!*

# Crazy Cran

## Ingredients

1 cup frozen cranberries
1 orange (peeled)
2 leaves collard greens
1 bunch mixed baby greens
3–4 mint leaves
1 pear
1 cup coconut water
1 lemon (juiced)
1 banana (optional)

Add first 4 ingredients. Blend until smooth, adding water, lemon juice, and coconut water as necessary. Add fruit. Pulse-blend until desired consistency.

This is not your regular cranberry cocktail, no, sir. This veritable dynamo of vitamins has it all. A high source of fiber in both mixed baby greens and collard greens with mint offering healthful digestive properties and cranberries providing bacteria blockers.

No jug of juice offers even a fraction of what Crazy Cran brings to the breakfast table. So blend up a glass and toast to your health.

# Mintal Melon

## Ingredients

4–5 mint leaves
1 bunch Chinese broccoli
¼ honeydew melon
½ cucumber
¼ cantaloupe
1 lime (juiced)

Add first 2 ingredients. Blend until smooth, adding water and lime juice as necessary. Add fruit. Pulse-blend until desired consistency.

*Clear your mind with this refreshing summer drink. Mint will sooth that upset stomach, put an end to that raging headache, and release a pleasant aroma that can calm even the craziest folks.*

*All the while the broccoli is silently engaged in a fight to the death with that extra cancer-inducing sunshine you're getting. You'd be mental not to give this one a try.*

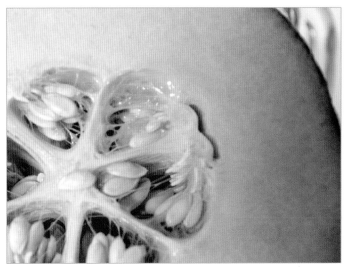

# Liquidate

## Ingredients

2 cups lamb's-quarters or
    dandelion greens
3–4 dates (pitted)
2 tbsp. raw almond butter
1 cup coconut water
1 cup frozen bluberries

Add first 2 ingredients.
Blend until smooth, add-
ing water and coconut wa-
ter as necessary. Add fruit
and almond butter. Blend
until desired consistency.

*You're going to hate when this one is gone.
Despite the bitter dandelion greens, the dates
do an awesome job at turning that bitter to
sweet bliss. You'll be purifying your liver and you
won't even know it. There's even healthy fats too.*

*Replace the blueberries with raspberries and
you'll have sweet, bitter, and sour all in one.*

# Guavacado

## Ingredients

1 cup guava
1 avocado
2 cups red leaf lettuce
1 cup mango
1 lemon (juice)
1 cup coconut water

Add all ingredients. Blend until smooth, adding water as necessary.

*Guavas can be hard to come by and vary quite drastically in size, shape, and texture. Test the seeds before you toss this one into the blender as some can be as hard as stones.*

*Also, some guava skin can be thick and bitter, so be sure to test that too. All this work just for a smoothie? You won't be disappointed once that creamy avocado texture hits your lips.*

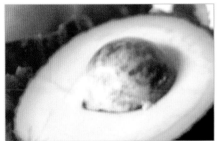

# Heavy Green

## Ingredients

1 cup broccoli
2 leaves collard greens
1 cup spinach
½ green apple
½ cucumber
½ avocado
1 lime (juiced)

Add all ingredients. Blend until smooth, adding water as necessary.

*Green-drink newbies need not apply; this one is for the hard-core green enthusiast. With minimal amounts of fructose, those with blood sugar issues will rejoice at this offering. Spinach, broccoli, and collards!*

*Top it of with the superfood avocado and you'll be brimming with a cancer-fighting, nutrient-dense glow. A savory treat not to be missed.*

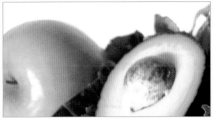

# Hit Pearade

## Ingredients

2–3 radish with tops
1 stalk celery
2 cups spinach
1 pear
1 cup pineapple
1 cup mixed berries
dash of cayenne

Add first 3 ingredients.
Blend until smooth, add-
ing water as necessary.
Add fruit and blend until
desired consistency.

*Look out! This one is spicy! The radish and
cayenne work together to prevent ulcers,
improve cardiovascular health, and clear those
clogged nasal passages right up.*

*The pineapple gives this spicy treat a vibrant
tropical flavor and increases energy levels
because of its high manganese and thiamin
content.*

*The pear offers just a hint of sweetness and is
the perfect amount to keep you from going up in
flames.*

# Jack Sprout

## Ingredients

3–4 Brussels sprouts
1 handful sunflower
   sprouts
½ grapefruit (peeled)
1 cup frozen jackfruit
1 lemon (juiced)
1 banana

Add first 4 ingredients.
Blend until smooth, add-
ing water as necessary.
Add fruit and blend until
desired consistency.

*Jack is one bitter dude. This is another one novices should run from. Jack Sprout is bitter, sour, and just perfect for the hard-core green-drinker. A vitamin C powerhouse, grapefruit also is a great source of prostate-cancer-fighting lycopene.*

*The brussels sprouts and sunflower sprouts add tremendous antioxidants and detox power. Jack ain't bitter no more, is he?*

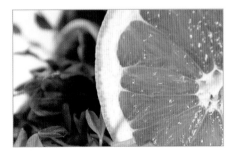

# American Pie

## Ingredients

2 green apples
2 cups spinach
1 cup young coconut flesh
1 banana
1 cup coconut water
cinnamon and nutmeg to
    taste

Add first 3 ingredients.
Blend until smooth, add-
ing water as necessary.
Add fruit and blend until
desired consistency.

*Dessert in a glass. I recommend green-weary kids give this one a go before jumping in to something less sweet. Fresh young coconut is one of the most delicious healthy fats available. Mixed with sweet apples and protein-rich spinach, this is the closest you'll get to eating something akin to Grandma's pie without passing out after eating.*

*The banana is not optional in this one; it increases the potassium content of the spinach and adds a creamy pie-like texture that'll have you coming back for more.*

# Lettuce Rock

## Ingredients

1 cup lettuce greens
1 cup rocket
1 cup mixed berries
1 banana
½ lime (juiced)

Add first 2 ingredients. Blend until smooth, adding water as necessary. Add fruit and blend until desired consistency.

*Simplicity. Sometimes you want nothing to interfere with the music, you know what I'm saying? Lettuce Rock is easy, cost effective to eat everyday, nutritious and delicious.*

*The mixed berries (I use frozen as it's even cheaper) add an antioxidant boost while the rocket (arugula) adds a nice bitter flavor that balances well with the sweetness of the banana and the tart of the lime. It's the perfect ensemble. Drink up, rock out.*

# Tom Soy-er

## Ingredients

2 Roma tomatoes
1 bunch Italian parsley
1 stalk celery
1 cup spinach
2 radishes with tops
Tabasco, black pepper, and
    soy sauce to taste

Add all ingredients. Blend until smooth, adding water as necessary.

*This peppery, salty, spicy tomato tonic will turn you into a modern-day warrior with a mean, mean stride. Parsley lends its tumor-fighting abilities and also helps increase the antioxidant capacity of the blood.*

*And if you're a smoker (why would you be?), it also helps neutralize certain types of carcinogens. It's our fresher version of V8 that won't leave you in a sodium coma.*

JUICES

# Rad-ish Radish

## Ingredients

2–3 kale leaves (remove
  stems)
¼ English cucumber
4 medium radish bulbs
  (with greens)
fresh ginger to taste
¼ cup water

Peel ginger root and juice
all, adding more water if
necessary.

*The spiciness of the radish and ginger are only slightly cooled down by the cucumber. A great drink to clear out the respiratory system or for those with seasonal allergies.*

*Add some bee pollen and double the allergy-fighting effects. You can even give it an Asian twist by substituting daikon radish for the standard red bulb.*

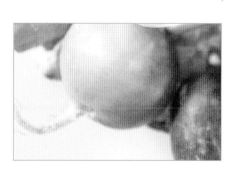

# Cool Slaw

## Ingredients

1 crown broccoli
½ small red cabbage
2 carrots
1 lemon (peeled)
1 green apple
ginger to taste

Peel ginger root and juice all. Serve over ice.

*A fresh-tasting summer delight perfect for parties by the pool, barbecues, and picnics at the park. Besides being the ideal accompaniment to any afternoon outside, Cool Slaw brings a lot to the picnic table.*

*Broccoli's cancer-fighting properties combat the carcinogens introduced to your meat from that smokey grill. Ginger works to settle stomachs and has long been a remedy for heartburn from those summer snacks. Serve with a few extra apples in your favorite punch bowl.*

# 4 Carrot Gold

## Ingredients

4 carrots
2 large kale leaves
1 bok choy bulb
1 golden apple
ginger to taste

Peel ginger root and juice all. Serve over ice.

*Rich, I say, Rich! Rich in vitamins, color, and in flavor, that is. Adding apple has always been a great way to balance out the grainy sweetness of carrots and still deliver the unbeatable shot of beta-carotene you get from them.*

*Bok choy's health-promoting compounds are better preserved when it is left uncooked, and what better way to maximize these rich health benefits. Break out the blender and have yourself a gold rush.*

# Red Queen

## Ingredients

2 kale leaves
1 medium beet
1 gala apple
¼ red cabbage
1 bunch red grapes

Juice.

*Long live the queen. Super sweet, sassy, and deep, dark red, Red Queen is one smart drink. Grape juice promotes brain health and memory function. Red cabbage is rich in iodine, which also promotes proper brain and nervous system function. One sip and you'll be singing the Red Queen's "Off with the cabbage head!" Just remember what the dormouse said, "Feed your head!"*

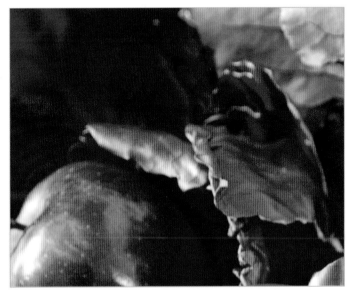

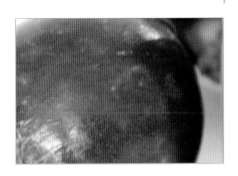

# Beetle Juice

## Ingredients

1 yellow bell pepper
1 Fuji apple
1 small crown broccoli
1 small beet
½ sweet potato
1 handful parsley
2 carrots

Juice.

*Saying it three times in succession may not raise the dead, but it will certainly raise your spirits and your energy levels. Bell pepper is a natural immune booster and coupled with broccoli, you've got yourself one helluva free-radical fighter. Eating sweet root vegetables like beets and sweet potato helps calm sugar cravings, so put down that donut and drink your veggies.*

# Hot Rocket

## Ingredients

2 Gala apples
2 handfuls of arugula
1 handful of cilantro
2 cups coconut water/
    milk
1 smidgen of jalapeño
    (to taste)
soy sauce to taste

Juice and mix with coconut water and soy sauce.

*This one is a bit different. We've got very bold and spicy flavors here. The coconut water, jalapeño, and salty soy sauce combine to give Hot Rocket a kind of Thai flavor while the cilantro brings back the Mexican flare.*

*Cilantro is also great for removing heavy metals from the bloodstream and jalapeños can raise your body temperature thereby increasing your metabolic rate. The healthy fats in the coconut milk will allow increase in mineral absorption from the arugula and cilantro.*

# Dande-Lemon

## Ingredients

1 bunch dandelion greens
1 bulb radicchio
ginger to taste
1 lemon (juiced, to taste)
dash cayenne

Juice and mix in cayenne.

*The ginger, lemon, and cayenne do a great job of taming the bitterness of the blood- and liver-purifying dandelion greens. This is like a suped-up lemonade. Master Cleanse aficionados will appreciate the lemon juice–cayenne pairing, which increases your body's fat-burning power and strengthens your immune system. Not much else to say except, it's really dandy.*

# Veggie-All

## Ingredients

1 beet
2 stalks celery
1 green bell pepper
1 large cucumber
lemon (juiced, to taste)
1 tsp. olive oil

Juice and mix (shake) with olive oil.

*Olive oil is a phytonutrient powerhouse and also helps the body absorb the many vitamins and minerals in the other vegetables.*

*You might want to play with the amount of green bell pepper here because sometimes the flavor can completely take over, or perhaps use a yellow or red pepper since they have a fruitier flavor. Sometimes I even add a couple of carrots to sweeten the lot.*

# Green King

## Ingredients

1 crown broccoli
1 green apple
1 bunch green grapes
2 handfuls spinach
2 large leaves collard
  greens

Juice.

*Where would we be without a solid green drink? I introduce you to a king and his crown . . . of broccoli?*

*Absolutely. Broccoli, the miracle food, packs the most nutritional punch of any vegetable, and it meets your complete fiber need providing both soluble and insoluble fiber. Green grapes are a natural antihistamine and despite their tiny stature, they really add quite a bit of sweetness. A juice fit for a king.*

# Rocket Fuel

## Ingredients

2 oz. (juiced) wheatgrass
   (or kale)
2 handfuls arugala
1–2 oranges (peeled)

Juice.

*All the energy and alertness provided by a shot of espresso without the shakes and eventual crash—this is what you can find in wheatgrass.*

*Wheatgrass is a high-alkaline, nutritionally dense green with a fairly potent flavor that some people have a hard time acclimating to; that's why you'll often find it paired with fresh orange slices at your local fresh juice bar. Not to mention it infuses the already high vitamin content with a significant amount of immune-boosting vitamin C.*

# Green Clean

## Ingredients

1 lime
1 lemon
1 large cucumber
1 handful basil
1 handful mint
2 handfuls spinach
ginger to taste

Juice.

*This one begs to be put into a giant ice-filled punch bowl and ladled into frosty glasses poolside. You'll never know your body is detoxifying as you gulp this delicious summer treat. Some folks may find it a bit too sour, so try adding an apple or two if that's the case.*

*Not only do we have great flavor, high amounts of vitamins, minerals, and antioxidants, Green Clean is one of the most aromatically appealing drinks in this book. Crisp, clean, refreshing.*

# Ginger Snap

## Ingredients

3–4 handfuls spinach
1 small anise bulb
ginger to taste
3–4 dates
1 cup frozen cherries
   (optional)

Juice spinach, anise, and ginger. Toss in a blender with dates and, for a Ginger Roy Rogers, add cherries. Blend. Serve over ice.

*This is practically a liquid dessert. Anise is great for digestion and paired with ginger, this drink is a perfect after-meal delight. The anise has a sophisticated licorice flavor that when paired with the sweetness of the dates makes for a dreamy combination.*

*The ginger adds a nice bite that helps steer you away from diabetic shock. Throw in a few frozen cherries to brighten it up or dare I say, add a scoop of sugar-free coconut ice cream for a float you won't soon forget.*

# Blimey Mary!

## Ingredients

2 medium tomatoes
2 celery stalks
1 bunch watercress
1–2 green onions (to taste)
1–2 carrots
1 lime (peeled)
Tabasco and pepper to
    taste

Juice. Add Tabasco and
pepper.

*A more savory flavor profile, the Blimey has heat, spice, and a double shot of nutrients. Celery, known as the zero-calorie vegetable, yields a sweet, savory, and slightly salty taste while the watercress and green onion spice it up a bit.*

*Tomatoes, the highlight of this drink, accounts for the slight sweet flavor and contains high levels of lycopene, known to fight against a list of cancers.*

*Add a dash of Tabasco for an extra kick and you've got a simple way to get that tomato juice taste without adding an unnecessary amount of sodium to your diet.*

# Cold Killah

## Ingredients

3–4 leaves purple kale
1 lemon (peeled)
ginger to taste
1 clove garlic
45–50 drops echinacea
2–3 carrots
1 sweet red bell pepper

Juice. Add echinacea and mix.

Packed with vitamin C, Cold Killah is the perfect cure or preemptive strike during cold season. Not only is echinacea known to boost the immune system, but so does the high amount of beta-carotene from both the carrots and red bell pepper.

Juicing to fight colds and illness is always a healthier and tastier alternative to those powdered cure packets any day. Sensing that tickle in your throat? Juice up a batch of Cold Killah, it'll stop that cold bug in its tracks.

# Gold 'n' Delicious

## Ingredients

2 golden delicious apples
1 kiwi (peeled)
2 cups chopped mustard
  greens
2 stalks celery
1 peach (pitted)

Juice.

Another dark green with heavy cancer-fighting properties, mustard greens have a spicier flavor profile than most others in the cruciferous family. Though these greens are often cooked, when juiced, their health benefits are amplified.

Toss in some sweet apples, peach, and kiwi to cut the spice and add a dose of vitamins and antioxidants and you've got yourself one delicious drink.

# Mint Julep

## Ingredients

1 stalk celery
1 handful mint leaves
2–3 handfuls spinach
1 apple

Juice.

You'd think it is summertime in a glass. Though its name might imply a less-healthy connotation, we can assure you this recipe will leave you refreshed and hopped up, but just on taste and vitamins. Celery and mint make for a smooth and clean taste while delivering essential nutrients and properties that are known to help lower blood pressure.

So kick back on the porch and enjoy. Bottoms up.

# Pome-ade

## Ingredients

1 cup fresh pomegranate
  juice
3–4 leaves beet greens
1 lemon (peeled)
1–2 cups red grapes

Juice.

*The fountain of youth is in your juicer. With age-fighting resveratrol in red grapes, the antioxidants heavy in pomegranate, and the LDL cholesterol-lowering elements of beet greens, you'll be looking good and feeling great as the years go by.*

*So sweet and tangy, this drink may convince you to trade in those face creams for a glass of Pome-ade. And remember, beauty comes from within.*

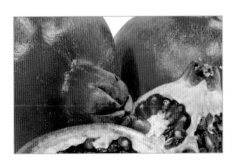

# Radicchio Active

## Ingredients

1 handful radicchio
2–3 radishes
1 lime (peeled)
1 cup chopped chard
1 green apple
2–3 carrots

Juice.

*A vitamin C powerhouse, Radicchio Active contains immune system-boosting properties to help wound healing and production of collagen. Chard, as well as providing anti-inflammatory effects, is also known to regulate blood sugar. Lime delivers a boost of calcium to the mix, and the detoxifying agents administered by the radishes help promote liver health.*

*All of these amazing elements combined may find you feeling like a superhero, without the radioactive spider bite.*

# Ener-Gee!

## Ingredients

1 orange (peeled)
1 apple
2–3 kale leaves
1 bunch watercress or 2
   oz. wheatgrass juice
2 cups spinach
2 carrots
1 small beet
ginger to taste

Juice.

*For those who like to start their day on all six cylinders, this drink is meant for you. None of those sugary, high-fructose corn syrup–laden, gas-inducing pick-you-up drinks can hold a candle to the energy one gets from just 2 oz. of fresh wheatgrass. Couple that with spinach, kale, beets, and you've got the healthier alternative to caffeine without the shakes and a dose of pure energy without the crash.*

*Don't have a masticating juicer? Substitute wheatgrass for watercress.*

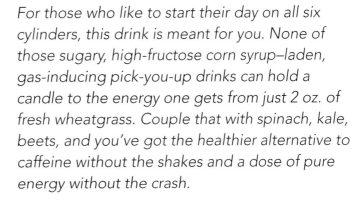

# Spring Sprout

## Ingredients

1–2 cups chopped brussels
   sprouts
1 lemon (peeled)
3–4 strawberries (leave
   tops on)
1 cup lettuce greens
1 orange (peeled)

Juice.

*Brussels sprouts tend to get a bad wrap. Every kid has pushed those pungent-smelling greens around their plate with a fork, hoping Mom or Dad might take pity and excuse them from the table before having to gulp them down. We can promise you'll have a change of heart in regard to brussels sprouts after trying Spring Sprout.*

*Its fruity-sweet taste will make you forget altogether that you're helping your immune system detox, fight cancer, and that you're actually eating your brussels sprouts. Make Mom proud and drink your sprouts.*

# Broccolean

## Ingredients

1 small crown broccoli
1 bunch parsley
4 carrots
1 medium cucumber

Juice.

An easier taste for a more seasoned juice-goer, Broccolean administers your daily dose of vegetables and helps to work your way to a slimmer figure and a healthier heart in just one glass.

Though carrots are high in sugar, they also provide a super jolt to the immune system, helping to fight illness and promote overall health. Parsley delivers a rich source of antioxidants, making this an all-around beauty beverage.

# Spiru-limade

## Ingredients

1 tbsp. spirulina powder
1 lime (peeled)
1 lemon (peeled)
1 bunch watercress
2 pears
1 nectarine

Juice.

*Spirulina, protein from the sea. Not only great for your body, spirulina helps prevent damage to brain cells and brain function and is perfect for vegans or vegetarians looking to get more protein in their diet. Capsules of this blue-green algae can be found in the supplements section of health and fitness stores near you, but be sure to invest in a well-trusted brand.*

*Mix contents of capsules into this tasty blend of sweet-and-sour vitamin-rich juice and feel the brain power surge.*

# Popeye Punch

## Ingredients

2 big bunches spinach
1 cup raspberries
2 cups pineapple

Juice.

This drink really packs a punch. Sweet, tart, and crammed with nutrients, Popeye Punch flexes heavy fiber, protein, and iron. Spinach, the most nutrient dense green, is essential to any growing kid or kid at heart's diet.

Better than powdered drinks, sodas, or cans of concentrated juice, Popeye Punch is the ideal drink for any kid of any age. Be strong to the finish and drink up your spinach.

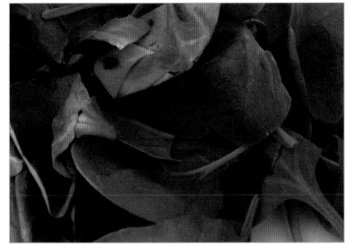

# True Collards

## Ingredients

4 leaves collards
2–3 cups watermelon
1 pear
1 cup bluberries
1 lime (peeled)

Juice.

You'll see your true colors shining through after introducing collards into your diet. More than likely, those colors will be varying shades of green. Pear and watermelon, high in vitamins K and C, add a sweet-sugary goodness to an often spicy-flavored green while blueberries and lime add antioxidants, tang, and dimension.

With a combination as sweet as this, we can certainly say, "It's easy being green."

# Greens Lover

## Ingredients

3 leaves kale
1 bunch cilantro
1 cup spinach
1 cucumber
1–2 carrots
1 green apple

Juice.

*The "good-for-you" factor in salads are oftentimes ruined by introducing dressings and oils, and you end up sacrificing health benefits for taste.*

*Not in the case of this drink. The fiber-rich kale and veritable powerhouse of vitamins that is spinach are paired with sweet carrots and a tart green apple juiced to a harmonious balance of taste and nutrition.*

*Who says you can't have it all?*

# Resources

The Encyclopedia of Healing Foods by Michael
  T. Murray, N.D.
www.hgdbook.com/healing-foods

The Coconut Oil Miracle by Bruce Fife, N.D.
www.hgdbook.com/coconut-miracle

User's Guide to Protein and Amino Acids (Basic
  Health Publications) by Keri Marshall, N.D.
www.hgdbook.com/amino-acids

The Protein Power Lifeplan by Michael R. &
  Mary Dan Eades, M.D.
www.hgdbook.com/protein-power

The Wheatgrass Book by Ann Wigmore
www.hgdbook.com/wheatgrass-book

Breville BJE510XL Ikon 900-Watt Variable-
  Speed Juice Extractor
www.hgdbook.com/juicer

Nutiva Organic Extra-Virgin
  Coconut Oil
www.hgdbook.com/nutiva

Tropical Traditions Gold Label Virgin Coconut
  Oil
www.hgdbook.com/coconut-oil

Sprout People—Sprouting supplies, kits and
  seeds
www.hgdbook.com/sprouts

Baker Creek Heirloom Seeds
www.hgdbook.com/heirloom

Amazing Grass Organic Wheat Grass Powder
www.hgdbook.com/wheatgrass-powder

The World's Healthiest Foods List
www.whfoods.com

USDA National Nutrient Database for
  Standard Reference
www.hgdbook.com/nutrient-data

www.nal.usda.gov/fnic/foodcomp/search/

SELF Nutrition Data
nutritiondata.self.com

About Organic Produce
www.hgdbook.com/organic-produce

Organic Foods vs Supermarket Foods:
  Element Levels by Bob L. Smith (Doctor's
  Data Inc.)
www.hgdbook.com/organic-vs-supermarket

Dietary Reference Intakes for Energy,
  Carbohydrate, Fiber, Fat, Fatty Acids,
  Cholesterol, Protein, and Amino Acids by
  the Food and Nutrition Board
www.hgdbook.com/dietary-intake

# Index